FOUNDATIONS OF FAITH

CHILDREN'S EDITION POCKET VERSION

ALL NATIONS INTERNATIONAL
TERESA SKINNER   GORDON SKINNER
AGNES I NUMER   ASHLEY FLORES

**Foundations of Faith
Children's Edition Pocket Version
Isaiah 58 Mobile Training Institute**

ISBN: 978-1-950123-66-7
Copyright © 2020 by All Nations International
All rights reserved.

*Unless otherwise indicated, all Scripture quotations are taken from the
Holy Bible, King James Version - Public Domain*

Cover Art: Julian Peter V. Arias and Eve Lorraine Rivers
Trinidad

Isaiah 58 Mobile Training Institute
is available for use in training programs.
For more information or to
order additional copies of this manual:

email: is58mti@gmail.com
contact us: www.all-nations.org
online course: is58mti.org

We dedicate this manual:
To those who wanted to know... but never had a teacher.
To those who looked for the vision... so that they could run with it.
To those who want to know "What's Next?"
To those who knew they were teachers... but did not know what to teach.
To those who are looking for Christ in Us the Hope of Glory!
May this manual reveal to you Jesus Christ and
May the peace that He has ordained for you be with you always.

CONTENTS

Who is God?	1
The Seventh Day	4
WHERE does God live?	5
WHERE does God live?	6
WHAT Color is God?	7
What does it mean to be created in God's Image?	9
WHO is God's One Enemy?	10
What Is Sin?	13
WHAT do we do if we SIN?	15
What is Repentance?	16
Who Is Jesus?	18
What Is Repentance?	23
What Is Salvation?	24
What Is Water Baptism?	27
Who is the Holy Spirit?	28
What is the Baptism of the Holy Spirit?	30
What Must I Do to Be Saved?	31
Go Make Disciples	33
Freely you have received, freely give	34
The Journey - Game Setup	35

WHO IS GOD?

WE THINK God is created like us... He is not… **We are created like Him.**

God was... Even before we were created. He has no beginning and no end. God made everything; heaven and earth and all living things. God also made man.

GOD IS THE CREATOR

In the beginning, God created the Heavens and the earth in only seven days:

Day 1: God created Light and separated the Light from the Darkness.
Day 2: God created the heavens.
Day 3: God created Earth, sea, and vegetation.
Day 4: God created Sun, Moon, and Stars.
Day 5: God created Birds and Sea Animals.
Day 6: God created Land Animals and Humans.
Day 7: God rested.

When God created man, he made him out of the dust of the earth. After God formed man, He breathed into him and man became a living, breathing creature. This makes us special to God.

Psalm 145:8, "The Lord is full of loving-favor and pity, slow to anger and great in loving- kindness."

God wants the best for you. The Bible is God's word written for man to understand His ways and His commands. **God is** merciful, gracious, slow to anger, abundant in loving kindness and truth.

After God created the world, He made a garden and put a man in it.

Imagine this place: the most beautiful garden, or park where there is no pain, suffering, or torment! Everything you need to eat grows naturally there for you. The animals get along peacefully. No one fights or is angry; there are no bad attitudes and no unkind words. God and His people walked and talked in the garden when the evenings became cool.

Everything was perfect.

This is what God made in the beginning, for the people He loved.

WHERE DOES GOD LIVE?

God lives in heaven and in our hearts.

God has His own kingdom.

God has His own culture and His own way of expressing Himself. We cannot control Him. He is God.

Draw a picture of God in Heaven

Draw a picture of God in your heart.

WHAT COLOR IS GOD?

God is Light, Light is all colors.

God is not white, brown, yellow, or black.

God is all colors. We are ALL made like Him.

It is important that we know who God is and that He wants to walk and talk with us.

God wants His people to know Him.

Scripture Memory: *Psalm 103:7. He made His ways known to Moses and His acts to the people of Israel.*

WHAT DOES IT MEAN TO BE CREATED IN GOD'S IMAGE?

When someone says, "You are like your Father," they are saying that you talk, walk, think and act like your Father, or that you have special abilities like he does. When God created us, He gave us special abilities and qualities like He has.

We have spiritual abilities to know God, to talk with Him, and to be aware of His presence.

We have free will – we can choose.

We have creativity – we can create.

We have intelligence – we can think, learn, and understand.

We have authority – we can rule (control, organize).

WHO IS GOD'S ONE ENEMY?

God has one enemy; he is evil and he hates God and hates His people. This enemy will do everything in his wicked power to stop God's plan. This enemy's name is Satan or the Devil.

He came to the Garden of Eden as a serpent, to lie to Adam and Eve. Adam and Eve listened to Satan and sinned. Then they could no longer walk and talk with God. The world became an ugly place to live because of sin.

God told them if they disobeyed, this would happen.. This is called "Death."

NOW, men are born with the tendency to sin… It is in their DNA.

People lost the strength to create or choose what is right, and they became slaves to sin. They are separated from God.

God wants you to become one of His children. God loves you and wants you to know Him and learn His ways. He will save you from the devil's lies and the bondage of sin. **God wants to restore** to you His special characteristics that He gave to Adam. **God wants to bring you back** into "the image of God." You will again be one of His people and **He will be your God.** You will learn to know Him, walk with Him, and talk with Him.

What is Sin?

Sin is:
Doing what we were not created to do.

Is what I am doing a sin?

WHAT IS SIN?

Ask yourself these questions:

- Is it something that God says is wrong?
- Does it make you sick or unhealthy?
- Do you always have to tell yourself it is right?
- Did you feel guilty/bad when you started doing it?
- Do you have to keep yourself from doing it?
- Is it sin?

SIN SEPARATES US FROM GOD.

God wants to bring us back to Him, so He can walk and talk with us like He did in the Garden of Eden with Adam and Eve.

WHAT ARE WE SUPPOSED TO DO ABOUT SIN?

- Run from sin!
- Say yes to God.
- Say no to the devil.
- Get close to God.
- Keep your heart clean.
- Make up your mind: No more!
- Ask God to forgive you from your sin.
- Let God into your life.

Draw a picture that shows what to do about sin:

WHAT DO WE DO IF WE SIN?

We must look at our sin the way God sees it.

We must repent.

WHAT IS REPENTANCE?

Feeling guilty is not repentance

Repentance is looking at the sin we have done... God's way. When we do, we become sorry for what we have done, and we don't do it again.
Sometimes, we have to run from sin.

WHAT IF WE ARE WEAK TO SIN?

The reason why God sent His only Son, Jesus, to die on the cross for us, is because we are weak to sin. When we ask God to forgive us, God gives us power over sin. This makes God happy!

SIN is also NOT DOING what we were created to do.

God gives us commands and instructions to follow for our own good. It is to make us into the person He created us to be. It is also to benefit others. When we do not obey God, it is sin.

Draw a picture of what has God asked you to do:

WHO IS JESUS?

We have all sinned, so now what can we do? Sin separates from the God who made us.

Sometimes we feel separated and must go on a journey to find God.

WHY are we separated from God?

God, the Creator of the Universe, walked with Adam and Eve in the garden.

Adam sinned. Adam's sin separated him and all of his descendants from God. **Adam and Eve became cursed and alone.**

WHO is Jesus?

Jesus is the Son of God.

Jesus is Emmanuel 'God on Earth.'

God sent Jesus to become **"The Ultimate Sacrifice." Jesus became** man to Save man.

Jesus became the sacrifice for our sins. Jesus died for our sins, so we didn't have to die without God.

Jesus not only washes away our sin, but takes from us all past, present, and future sins and works in our hearts that we may not continue to live in sin.

JESUS brought us back to God.

Jesus' ultimate sacrifice makes Him our Savior.

What Is Repentance?

WHAT IS REPENTANCE?

We now realize we have a problem. Sin has separated us from God.

How do we get to where God is taking us?

WHAT is the problem?

Because of Adam and Eve's sin, everyone born is separated from God!

WHAT is the Solution?

Repentance!

HUMAN REGRET is not repentance

We cannot just feel guilty when we do something wrong. We must ask for change so we don't continue to sin. We must have godly sorrow.

GODLY SORROW – Godly sorrow leads to doing something about the situation.

Do you have something that you would like to repent from?

Have you asked Jesus the Ultimate Sacrifice to come into your heart and give you a new life? Have you found yourself ignoring sin and instead doing what you think is right and not looking to what God says is right? Maybe you would like to pray and ask Him for forgiveness. Begin that new life right now.

WHAT IS SALVATION?

Salvation – the gift that comes through accepting Jesus Christ, the "Ultimate Sacrifice," who brings us back to God, back to who we were created to be, and to Heaven when we die.

WHY do we need Salvation?

God, the Creator of the Universe, walked with Adam and Eve in the Garden.

Adam sinned. Adam's sin separated him and all of his descendants from God.

What is salvation?

Jesus died for your sins.

Ask Him to forgive you of your sins. Ask Him to be the King of your heart.

WHEN JESUS ANSWERS YOUR PRAYER, THIS IS WHAT HAPPENS:

Scripture memory: *I will give you a new heart and put a new spirit within you. I will take away your heart of stone and give you a heart of flesh. And I will put My Spirit within you and cause you to follow My laws and be careful to do what I tell you.*

Ezekiel 36:26-27

Do you have a new heart? Draw your heart:

WHAT IS WATER BAPTISM?

Water baptism is when a believer is immersed underwater, symbolize Jesus dying and raising to new life.

Through water baptism, Jesus says to Satan, "**No longer** will you have control over them. When they go down into that water with Me, **everything** that you have in them is gone.

You come up out of that water with new life, you come out a new creature, and you come out a **son of God.**

Join Jesus in burial through water baptism:

- Destroys the DNA – (the sin nature) of Adam.

- Replaces the DNA – (the new nature) of Jesus Christ.

Through water baptism we are no longer slaves to sin, but we are servants of righteousness.

God has given us the answer.

WHO IS THE HOLY SPIRIT?

Our God is three persons, but one God. The Father, Jesus His Son, and The Holy Spirit.

The Holy Spirit was active in creating the Earth and writing the Bible.

The Holy Spirit loves to teach people about God. He will comfort you when you feel sad.

Holy Spirit loves to help you when you ask him.

What is the Baptism of the Holy Spirit?

But you shall receive power
when the Holy Spirit has come upon you;
and you shall be witnesses to Me in Jerusalem, and
in all Judea and Samaria, and to the end of the earth."
Acts 1:8

What is the Baptism of the Holy Spirit?

After Jesus was killed, he was dead for three days, then His Father made Him come alive again. Then He went back to heaven to be with His Father. Before Jesus went to heaven, he spent 40 days with his students. He promised to send the Holy Spirit to be with them so they would not be alone.

After Jesus left, The Holy Spirit came to Jesus' students who were together praying, and He baptized them with power and boldness. It was such an amazing experience. They began boldly preaching about Jesus in languages they had never learned and made sick people well.

Now they would not be afraid or alone because the Holy Spirit came to live inside of them, so He was always with them.

Jesus' promise is for you too! You can have the baptism of the Holy Spirit too if you ask Him.

WHAT MUST I DO TO BE SAVED?

Pray this prayer:

Dear Jesus, I know that I have sinned; I have chosen to do things that are wrong when I could have chosen the right way. I repent from those sins; I want and need my life to change... Today. Please forgive me and place your new heart and your new spirit within me. Please come and live in my heart forever. Jesus, please fill my heart with your love and compassion for others and guide me all of the days of my life. Amen.

Now, look for a church that believes in the Bible as the Word of God. Find out what the next steps are to be a Christian, follow Jesus, know God as your King, and be led by His Spirit.

HOW can we protect such a great gift?

Spend good time with God and other Believers

Walk in the Light

Keep confessing your sins

Spend time reading your Bible

Pray daily

Go Make Disciples

"Go, preach, teach, and baptize
and make disciples of all nations."
Matthew 28:19, Mark 16:15-16.

GO MAKE DISCIPLES

A disciple is a follower or student of a teacher.

When Jesus called his disciples, he simply said, "Follow me and **I will make you** fishers of men" Matthew 4:19.

Jesus taught them to do everything He did, to heal every kind of sickness, cast out devils, and preach about the Kingdom of Heaven.

Just before Jesus went to heaven, He told His disciples to tell the whole world the good news.

BUT, How can you follow a God you cannot see?

Follow the Bible. This is our instruction book to teach us what is right. It is God's letter to us.

Follow the Holy Spirit who gives us personal direction since He lives inside of us now.

It is natural for you to hear God's voice and be led by the Holy Spirit.

God loves people so much that Jesus died for them. He wants you to tell people and make disciples of those who will believe your words.

Scripture Memory. "Go, preach, teach, and baptize and make disciples of all nations."

Matthew 28:19, Mark 16:15-16.

FREELY YOU HAVE RECEIVED, FREELY GIVE.

Scripture Memory: *Matthew 28:19 Go ye therefore, and teach all nations, baptizing them in the name of the Father, and of the Son, and of the Holy Ghost: 20 Teaching them to observe all things whatsoever I have commanded you: and, lo, I am with you always, [even] unto the end of the world.*

The Journey - Game Setup

YOU NEED:

- Number cards or Dice

- Bottle caps or other small objects – 1 per player

You can make them:

- Make 3 sets of cards, number them from 1-3. Or make paper dice - see pictures on opposite page.

- Place 1 small coin, bottle cap or other object on the start space – per player.

Object of the Game:

The first player to go from START to FINISH wins. You can only reach there by

an exact count.

Game Play

On your turn a player must:

- Draw a card or roll the paper dice and move the amount of squares on the card

- If you reach the FINISH square and have too many moves you must move backward.

- Two or more players may stop on a square at the same time.

- The first player to get the bottle cap on the FINISH square wins the game!

How to make Paper Dice:

1. Photocopy this page - there are two die here to let you practice.

2. Cut the die out along its outside border.

3. Fold the die along each of the six sides (along the lines).

4. With small pieces of clear tape, tape each edge to another edge. ...

5. Roll the die to see if it works, then play the game!!

Make a copy of these cards and cut out 3 sets.

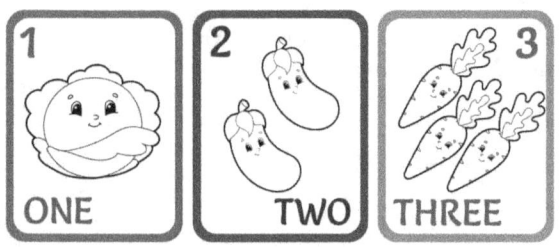

Shuffle them and draw a card. Move the amount of spaces on the card.

www.ingramcontent.com/pod-product-compliance
Lightning Source LLC
Chambersburg PA
CBHW052128110526
44592CB00013B/1793